Marketing

A Good Practice Guide

London: The Stationery Office

Prepared by the Further Education Development Agency and
KPMG Management Consulting

**THE
FURTHER
EDUCATION
FUNDING
COUNCIL**

**Department for
Education and Employment**

Preface

The contents of this guide are based on an investigation into marketing in further education colleges, conducted by the Further Education Development Agency (FEDA) and KPMG Management Consulting. Commissioned jointly by the Further Education Funding Council (FEFC), the National Audit Office (NAO), the Department for Education and Employment (DfEE), and with the support of the Further Education Funding Council for Wales (FEFCW), this exercise was designed to identify examples of effective marketing practice which support efforts by colleges to improve student recruitment, retention and achievement.

FEDA and KPMG consultants visited 15 colleges. Using audit techniques, they researched key issues in interviews with a cross-section of staff. Participating colleges were placed in four groups: the North East, North West, East Midlands and South East regions of England, with the addition of one college in Wales. Fieldwork was carried out during October and November 1996.

Background material from the 15 colleges was supplemented where appropriate by examples from other institutions known to the FEDA–KPMG project team. The guide also draws on evidence from another NAO study, *Further Education Colleges in England: Strategies to achieve and manage growth*, as well as on a range of other published sources which are listed in the bibliography in annex D.

Good Practice Guides

The FEFC and the NAO have commissioned a series of good practice guides which offer guidance and practical advice for further education colleges and others on various aspects of college management. The publications currently available in this series are:

Estate Management in Further Education Colleges: A Good Practice Guide (HMSO 1996; price £13.95)

Procurement: A Good Practice Guide (TSO 1997; price £15.95)

Effective Facilities Management: A Good Practice Guide (TSO, 1997; price £16.95)

A Good Practice Guide on using consultancy services is in preparation.

Contents

HM Treasury has recommended the following guidelines to public sector organisations to ensure regularity and propriety in the handling of public funds.

■ Don't bend or break the rules

■ Put in place and follow clear procedures

■ If approval is needed, get it first

■ Don't allow a conflict of interests to affect, or appear to affect, decisions

■ Don't use public money for private benefit

■ Be even-handed

■ Record the reasons for decisions

Chapter 1

The Relevance of Marketing to Further Education

Introduction

1.1   Effective marketing has always been vital for colleges. The terminology associated with it might have seemed alien, and the interpretation narrower than is usual in the business world, but colleges have always sought to secure the best match between the curriculum, the customer and business needs. This was true even before incorporation, and since then, the emphasis on raising the profile of further education, widening participation and securing sound college finances has enhanced the importance of effective marketing still further.

1.2   Changes in funding in 1997, far from signalling a decline in marketing activity, have also contributed to its importance. The focus may have shifted from rapid growth across the board to more limited growth in key priority areas, improving retention, achievement and progression and increasing the income from employers, but effective marketing is every bit as crucial in this new context.

1.3   Over recent years, there has been a rising level of interest and enthusiasm for the application of business marketing principles in further education. This chapter presents a working definition of marketing, and looks at how marketing principles in the business sector can contribute to the marketing function in colleges, which are seen essentially as service providers.

Policy Considerations

1.4   The following key issues need to be taken into consideration.

- ensure that marketing contributes to the strategic and financial planning process, and to the achievement of the college's objectives and business viability

- use the marketing function as a means of seeing the college from the customer's viewpoint, and act accordingly

- match capacity and demand

- use effective market segmentation

- use differentiated marketing approaches

- develop an efficient quality assurance system across all aspects of the organisation

- aim for a high level of repeat business from existing satisfied customers

- establish an effective and compelling corporate identity and external image

- involve all staff in the marketing process, since contact with staff at all levels is vitally important in influencing customer opinions

- monitor the results, and evaluate the cost-effectiveness of individual promotional activities.

Guidance

What is Marketing?

1.5   The Chartered Institute of Marketing has defined marketing as 'the management function responsible for identifying, anticipating and satisfying customer requirements at a profit.' In further education, marketing can be interpreted as the means by which college senior managers use a sustained and thorough knowledge of present and future markets to ensure that strategic planning addresses the education and training needs of customers cost-effectively. Figure 1 is a diagrammatic representation of the suggested definition of marketing.

Figure 1. What is marketing?

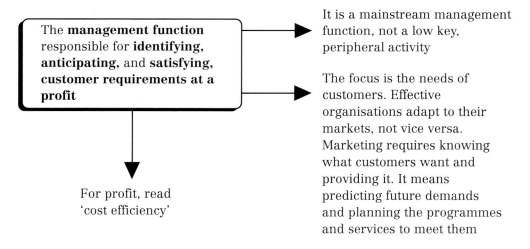

The **management function** responsible for **identifying, anticipating,** and **satisfying, customer requirements at a profit**

It is a mainstream management function, not a low key, peripheral activity

The focus is the needs of customers. Effective organisations adapt to their markets, not vice versa. Marketing requires knowing what customers want and providing it. It means predicting future demands and planning the programmes and services to meet them

For profit, read 'cost efficiency'

1.6   A further consideration for college managers is that merely being responsive to expressed market needs might not be consistent with a mission which identifies the college's active contribution to, for example, the promotion of widening participation or inclusive learning. College marketing needs to strike a balance between being responsive and seeking actively to stimulate demand.

Marketing a Service: Pointers from Business

1.7   College marketing differs from that employed in the private sector in that profit is not the primary aim of the organisation. Although this difference between the private and public sectors exists, college managers can nevertheless learn from the marketing function outside education. Just as in the private sector, there is constant pressure on colleges to maintain sound finances and operate cost-effectively.

1.8   The three-way relationship between marketing, curriculum planning and resourcing is the key to effective strategic planning and management. Part of the marketing agenda has to be to identify and promote activities which the college knows will add up to a programme which is financially viable as well as educationally sound. Strategic planning is assumed, throughout this guide, to incorporate financial planning.

1.9   Colleges primarily provide services, not products. In other service sectors, marketing with maximum impact is usually characterised by:

- a clear strategic view of marketing

- marketing intelligence which is useful and used

- targeted approaches to each different customer group

- service development linked to market information and feedback

- an effective sales operation

- a strong corporate identity

- effective marketing organisation

- regular monitoring and evaluation of marketing activities.

Each of these considerations is discussed in greater detail in the chapters that follow.

Conclusions

1.10   Colleges need to apply the principles of good marketing practice to the particular context in which they work. Principals and those responsible for strategic planning should develop a clear and coherent strategic view of marketing which will fully support the college strategic plan, help achieve its objectives and maintain business viability. Market intelligence requires targeted approaches to each customer group and should be capable of forecasting demand as well as contributing to an efficient quality assurance system and informing curriculum and resource development. An effective sales operation and strong corporate identity, supported by staff at all levels, will contribute to an effective marketing function, and will help support the principle of service quality.

Chapter 2

A Strategic View of Marketing

Introduction

2.1   Marketing is a critical part of the process by which the college strategy is formulated and carried forward. Through the information it contains, the marketing plan informs the college strategic plan and is an integral part of the strategic planning process. Together, the marketing and strategic plans spell out what people in the college will do to fulfill the college's mission.

2.2   This chapter examines the relationship between the marketing and strategic plans, and shows how the productive use of marketing can help to shape and support the college mission.

Policy Considerations

2.3   The following key issues need to be taken into consideration.

- firm leadership will provide an unwavering sense of purpose and a clear vision which is communicated and understood throughout the organisation

- strategic thinking needs to be supported by a constant and accurate flow of information on markets

- there is a balance to be struck between responding to increases and decreases in demand and maintaining or opening up new markets in line with the college mission

- the marketing and strategic plans should be closely related

- marketing should be recognised as a strategic responsibility of the college corporation and senior management, not just something to delegate to a marketing unit.

Guidance

College Mission and Ethos

2.4   Each college's marketing plan should be tailored to the mission, which in turn reflects the needs of the local community and the people served by the college. A key factor in achieving clarity in the college mission is the principal, and the leadership he or she provides.

2.5   The principal can encourage an institutional culture where the 'ownership' of strategy spreads through the organisation as a whole, and where curriculum leaders and other colleagues feel able to contribute at a strategic level. With responsibility comes the fostering of a 'can do' spirit amongst staff, encouraging innovation and learning from experience when some risks do not pay off.

2.6   Many mission statements indicate a commitment to quality assurance, and the principal may lead here by demonstrating this: genuine and continuing review, and an all-pervasive regard for the needs of customers, rather than vested interests, are two important ways of doing so.

Leadership creates a marketing culture

CASE STUDY

At several colleges visited during the fieldwork stage of the study, the sense of purpose and enthusiasm was almost tangible: a powerful impression of staff sharing a common purpose; a belief in the college's aims and achievements, showing confidence in the 'brand'; an unswerving pursuit of quality in every aspect of the organisation; a reliance on flexible teamwork within a coherent and widely understood structure; and delegation of responsibility — even risk — to those staff best placed to judge the context and act accordingly.

In some colleges, the study team was very impressed by the willingness to question and challenge long-established assumptions (an example was the determination of one college to unravel the issues beneath the concept — often turned to cliché — of 'multi-skilling') and to home in on the key priorities within an overall strategy of change.

What prompted such approaches were the working style and philosophy of senior management teams and, beyond that, the convictions, vision and energy of the principal. There are as many different ways of doing this as there are principals and senior managers involved, and the 'how' is very much a matter of personal leadership style. But without some form of effective strategic leadership, marketing will founder.

Marketing Supports Strategic Planning

2.7   Figure 2 is a diagrammatic representation of the relationship that exists between the design and delivery of the curriculum and the following four factors which exert an influence upon curriculum planning:

- the organisation's mission

- the requirements of potential markets and stakeholders

- the available resources

- the staff working for the organisation.

All these are subject to the influence of local and national environments.

Figure 2. Marketing as an element of strategic thinking

Local and national environment

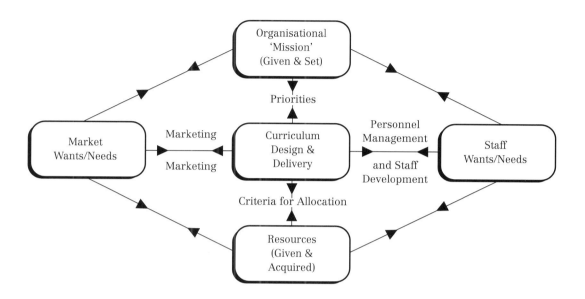

2.8 The design and delivery of the curriculum sits at the centre of figure 2, rightly, since it is the core business of colleges. Curriculum planning encompasses more than just the courses the college runs — it is the whole way in which the college manages the student learning experience from enquiry to completion, and includes advice and guidance, learner and learning support, as well as the programmes on offer.

A marketing view of the curriculum

A major airline achieved a significant turn-round in their business success by redefining their 'product' from providing flights to being a customer service organisation. Many colleges are achieving a similar transformation by taking a market-led view of the curriculum. This is defined as the whole portfolio of college services making up the student learning experience. This broadens the debate from 'what courses should we put on?' to 'how should we be supporting our students in their learning?'

2.9 Beyond this, good practice in marketing suggests that the curriculum itself should be determined primarily by the requirements of those the college seeks to serve. From this, it is clear that effective marketing plays a key role in informing the organisational mission and priorities for future direction, in determining the criteria for the allocation of existing resources and the acquisition of new ones, and in shaping staff development, recruitment and other personnel policies.

Responsive and Proactive Marketing

2.10   Similarly, marketing is most effective when it is responsive to a college's mission, capturing a sense of what the college is striving to achieve, in addition to the way in which it sees itself. Colleges with, for example, a clear commitment to increasing participation by under-represented communities, or improving the skill levels in the local workforce, have a strong focus to lead their marketing which takes them beyond simply responding to an articulated demand for education and training into developing new partnerships with their local communities.

Responding to changing community needs

A Yorkshire college found its vocational base suffering from the decline of the local mining industry. They responded by developing new programmes which would be suitable for the needs of the newly unemployed local men, taking advantage of regional funding. The college is responding to significant cultural changes, including the problem of falling self-esteem in men which has created significant barriers to access. Part of the college response has been to develop appropriate marketing approaches to break down these barriers. Initiatives include promoting programmes at local sporting venues, and using mature male staff to lead programmes and marketing.

Resources

2.11   In drawing up information on the resource implications of courses to inform marketing, colleges will need to calculate:

- target and forecast levels of recruitment

- possible funding sources and the estimated funds available from each source

- resourcing needs of staffing and staff development, research, materials, accommodation and publicity

- a unit cost for delivering each course

- a cashflow projection for each course.

2.12   Financial guidelines for each of these are needed. Course costing, for example, is not a simple matter and certainly not one which curriculum managers can perform without a clear framework and cost data. Some colleges have developed models to help curriculum managers cost their courses consistently. Most of these models are based on that set out in *Unfinished Business* (Audit Commission, 1993) and reproduced in figure 3.

Figure 3. The key elements of a course costing approach

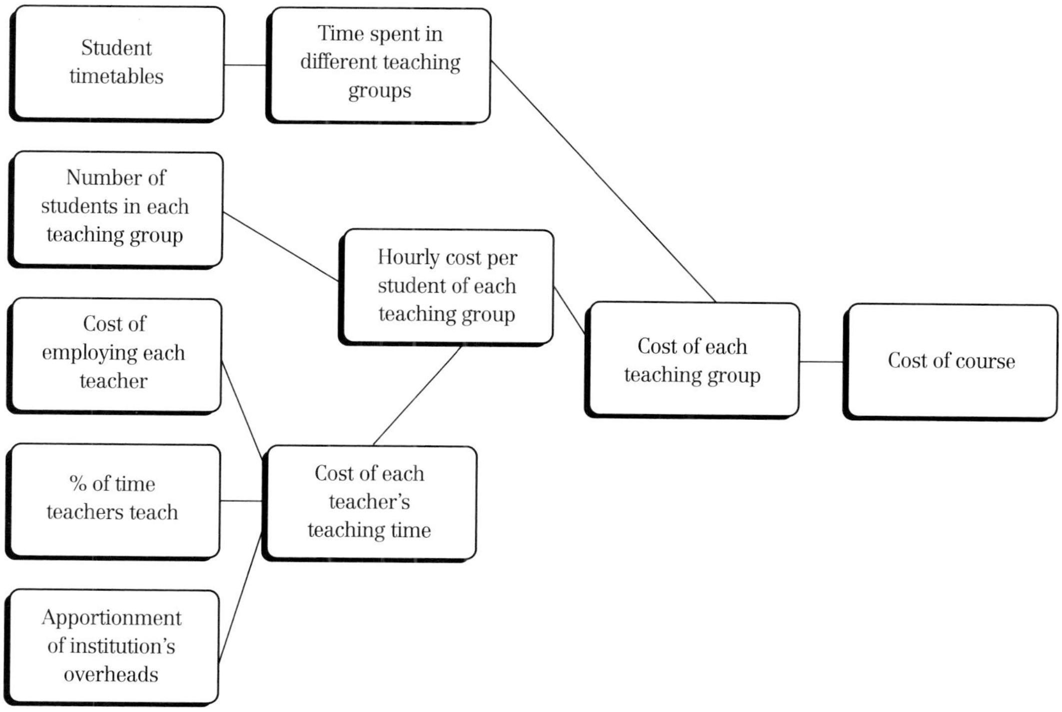

The only data which the approach requires are readily available

2.13   Planning decisions require a thorough understanding of market trends, how other providers are likely to react, and how the organisation's capabilities and strengths are mirrored by others and viewed by its own users. If the information is unavailable, but clearly necessary, then it is right to commission targeted research, once it is clear that the outcome merits the investment in value-for-money terms.

2.14   Nevertheless, it is still important to judge the proper balance between comprehensive marketing information and information overload, which can mean that action is stifled. This is sometimes referred to colloquially as 'paralysis by analysis'.

Marketing Plans

2.15   The marketing plan needs to be matched to a sound business analysis to create a curriculum portfolio which is viable both in terms of student recruitment and the college's ability to deliver and finance it.

2.16   A marketing plan is invaluable in ensuring that marketing staff are clear about operational priorities. Where such a plan is divorced from the overall mission and strategic plan there is an unacceptable risk that marketing will fail to inform the college's developing strategic vision.

2.17   There are no hard and fast rules about what a marketing plan should look like, but the following extracts should serve as a guide. Some elements, such as the overall aims and strategic analysis, will be common to the marketing and the strategic plans. Others will appear in much more detail in the marketing plan, such as objectives and targets for marketing, the marketing mix and its rationale, and the marketing action plan. Exactly how the marketing and strategic plans are written will depend on what the college wants to use them for, and is a matter of circumstances and judgement. The example in figure 4 is adapted from *Marketing Plans: How to prepare them, how to use them* (MHB McDonald, 1995).

Figure 4. Contents of a marketing plan

- Statement of overall corporate aims and values, and key objectives for the planning timescale as set out in the strategic plan.

- Situation analysis: an evaluation of the external environment and the internal capabilities of the college to clarify strengths and weaknesses, opportunities and threats (SWOT analysis).

- Specific marketing objectives together with measurable targets for their achievement.

- Adjustments to the marketing mix designed to achieve these objectives.

- Action programme: what needs to be undertaken, responsibilities for their accomplishment (who), timescales (when) and resources (money and time).

- Evaluation and review: the targets, performance indicators and other criteria against which progress towards the achievement of the objectives will be judged and decisions taken on appropriate remedial action. The outcomes of the evaluation and review process are also used to inform the basis for the next strategic plan, and for the next marketing planning cycle.

2.18 This can be compared with the similar approach proposed by The Chartered Institute of Marketing:

- mission statement
- financial summary
- market overview
- SWOT analysis
- portfolio summary
- assumptions
- marketing objectives and strategies
- programmes with forecasts and budgets.

Marketing as a Strategic Responsibility

2.19 The KPMG–FEDA study emphasised that the 'healthiest' colleges are characterised by a clear strategic vision and strong sense of direction. What is apparent, too, is the importance of a thorough understanding of the significance of marketing throughout the college and, within that, the need for a determinedly sustained customer focus. College managers need to be committed to the marketing focus, rather than regarding it as peripheral.

2.20 Principals and senior management teams in the more successful institutions regularly devote time and attention to marketing issues. While it may not be necessary for responsibility to be flagged in a senior manager's formal job title, there is real value in ensuring that responsibility for the marketing function rests with someone at a senior level. This should ensure that the perspective which comes from an informed overview is properly represented within the senior management team, and that marketing is more likely to be regarded as one of the key functional areas essential to the strategic planning process, rather than a separate and isolated unit confined to the operational.

2.21 Finally, there is also real value in engaging corporation members in the college marketing plan and in contributing to marketing activities. Most corporation members bring a wealth of experience of the communities the college serves and this is a vital resource. Their legal responsibility for the educational character and mission of the college also means that a strategic overview of marketing, in terms of the groups the college seeks to serve, is very much part of their business.

CHECKLIST

This checklist is intended to assist with the review and action planning process.

		Yes	No	Action needed
a.	Are curriculum leaders involved in strategy development?	☐	☐	☐
b.	Is there a 'can do' spirit among staff?	☐	☐	☐
c.	Do the senior management team and corporation board have a top-level commitment to quality assurance and customer focus?	☐	☐	☐
d.	Is the available marketing information fit for purpose?	☐	☐	☐
e.	Is the corporation board using marketing information to inform the mission and priorities?	☐	☐	☐
f.	Is the senior management team using market information to inform the curriculum offer?	☐	☐	☐
g.	Is the senior management team using market information to inform decisions about resource allocation and resource needs?	☐	☐	☐
h.	Is the senior management team using market information to inform staffing and staff development?	☐	☐	☐
i.	Is there a clearly spelled out mission about impact on the community, not just the college?	☐	☐	☐
j.	Has the marketing manager produced a costed marketing plan with operational priorities?	☐	☐	☐
k.	Is there consistency of priorities across the marketing plan and the strategic plan?	☐	☐	☐
l.	Do the members of the senior management team devote time to marketing activity?	☐	☐	☐
m.	Is there clear responsibility for marketing at a senior level?	☐	☐	☐

Chapter 3

Environmental Analysis and Market Research

Introduction

3.1   Colleges need to be closely in touch with their markets through accurate and timely market information. To identify and consolidate that knowledge, it is necessary to keep the performance of the college under continuing review and to probe the key characteristics of the communities it serves. Without that kind of information — targeted, focused and relevant — marketing planning becomes an act of faith, not a logical reaction to circumstances and perceived trends.

Policy Considerations

3.2   The following key issues need to be taken into consideration.

- an overall picture of potential markets may be drawn from a variety of sources and integrated within the management information system

- the acquisition and use of available external data is important when researching markets

- working with partners, including TECs, local authorities and LEAs, will generate new data focused on college needs

- student tracking information is useful for informing marketing plans

- gather and use qualitative market information, and use staff knowledge and contacts

- conduct effective market research

- allocate an appropriate budget for marketing research.

Guidance

Market Research

3.3   The following discussion will help colleges ensure that the provision of market research is adequate, and that the college is well-placed to make judgements in the light of contextual information.

3.4   Effective market research usually forms part of an integrated marketing management information system. Figure 5 illustrates a typical approach adopted by a private sector trading organisation.

Figure 5. A marketing management information system

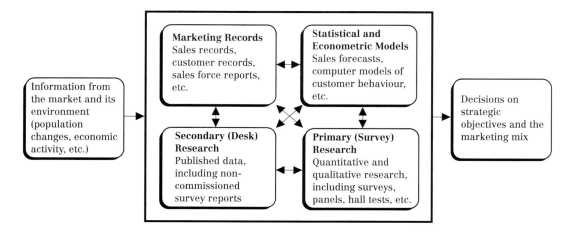

3.5   In the further education context:

- **information from the market**   includes local demographic data, labour market information (LMI), post-16 enrolment figures at colleges and with other providers

- **marketing records**   include student tracking data and enquiry logging

- **statistical models**   might include course enrolment projections based on statistical trends

- **primary research**   includes any new surveys commissioned by the college, for example in new geographical areas or among under-represented groups, student feedback questionnaires, student perception of course (SPOC) and employer perception of course (EPOC) analyses

- **secondary research**   includes TEC and government office data.

Acquiring external data

3.6   The following list gives some of the main sources of data on which the college might draw in order to inform its marketing strategy.

- **employer databases of corporate clients**   a useful starting point can be a commercial database, for example from the *Yellow Pages*, which can subsequently be adapted to the college's particular needs. The data need to be kept up to date, but can be invaluable in ensuring the precise targeting of publicity materials. Accessibility is important too, not least for ease of interrogation for staff preparing for a meeting with a local employer

- **pupil and school-leaver information**   published by the DfEE down to regional level and by local authorities. The careers service also regularly supplies information on the destinations of school-leavers. The numbers in each year at school are known and so are the trends on leaving compulsory education in terms of the split between staying on at school, entering further education and training, entering employment or other choices. Thus, colleges can predict their potential take-up from this market segment with a fair degree of precision

- **population census**   produced every 10 years (the most recent is 1991) and containing information about the population broken down by enumeration districts (EDs) which contain up to 200 households and which can be amalgamated to provide data by postcode. Local authorities and TECs normally hold census data for their own area

- **unemployment count**   released monthly and available from the local office of the Employment Service or the TEC

- **employment census and annual employment survey**   conducted annually by the DfEE and published at district level, though data relating to wards is usually available from the local authority or the TEC. This comprises:

  — vacancy data available by TEC areas from the local TEC or Employment Service

  — labour force survey published quarterly, providing information by districts and TEC areas

  — population projections produced at national level by the Office for National Statistics; local authorities often derive projections from these figures for districts or wards. Local authority planning departments usually hold such data

- **postcode data**   the Responsive College Unit (RCU) is one of several providers of computerised systems to map such data. Analysis of such data can reveal:

  — patterns of enrolment by location

  — recruitment by market segment in various locations

  — where enrolment is highest and lowest (the RCU's Scenario service is useful for this)

  — the characteristics of areas of successful recruitment

  — differences in recruitment area compared with that of other providers

- **analysis of other providers**   working in collaboration and partnership can include a realistic appraisal of other providers — other colleges, schools with sixth forms and private training providers. Sources of information on these include brochures, prospectuses and price lists, FEFC and OFSTED inspection reports, annual reports and financial statements, and examination and qualification statistics. There is also merit in establishing how other providers propose to respond to changes in the market-place

- **commissioned research**   primary research of this kind, where new information is sought from a target population, is more expensive than the other examples of market research cited here. Investment of this kind needs to be made with caution, with clear evidence that the outcomes warrant the cost. However, many colleges do carry out regular surveys of students and employers to inform their marketing and quality plans. Costs can be reduced if local partners work jointly.

Database marketing

3.7   With the increased availability of computer-based systems, many more organisations now engage in the statistical analysis of data in order to develop a better understanding of the way in which their markets work. Customer records are analysed, so data are collected by primary research. In particular, there have been considerable advances in the techniques of direct marketing (also known as database marketing). Many of these techniques are based on geodemographics — the profiling of market and customer records by postcode and enumeration district. Consumption patterns for all goods and services within a given geographical area can be segmented into small groups of households possessing distinct features with a high degree of accuracy. By profiling its own customers, and matching the customer profile against that for the whole population in a particular catchment area, an organisation can identify specific postcodes with the most and least potential for targeting, thereby assisting in the improvement of its promotional and other marketing activities.

3.8   The parallel in further education would be the college which analyses its enrolment, retention and achievement patterns by, say, postcode, age, sex and previous education or employer to identify in which areas the college strategies are most or least successful. This kind of analysis will be particularly important in responding to the priority of widening participation: the starting point is identifying under-participating groups, and examining the potential for improving recruitment, retention, achievement and progression.

3.9   Other more sophisticated techniques include looking for partner organisations with customer lists that are likely to be similar to the college's in order to share databases. For example, a college might identify that many of its students also hold and use local authority leisure cards, and vice versa, and swap lists with the local authority to gain new targets, although it is not easy keeping up to date. BT estimates that commercial information on customer lists becomes outdated at a rate of more than 20 per cent a year. Colleges will need to ensure that their existing registrations under the *Data Protection Act*, especially the purposes for which the data are being held, are sufficient to meet these marketing needs. In general, data provided for one purpose, for example, student registration, may not be used for another, for example, general marketing, without the consent of the data subject. Colleges may wish to ensure that their data providers are legally empowered to provide such data.

Working with partners

3.10   Successful colleges are working with other partners in the local communities to share research and information on local markets. For example, several colleges have built very effective working relationships with their local TECs, asking the TEC to include particular questions relevant to the college in future surveys of local labour markets and trends. This tactic of 'piggy-backing' on other work can be a cost-effective approach to gathering information.

Working with the TEC to generate targeted information

CASE STUDY

Both local and national labour market information (LMI) point to an ageing workforce in agriculture. One specialist agriculture college was particularly keen to get a clear local picture on the age factor. The local TEC operates a number of industry-specific panels to advise the TEC board. There is some cross-membership between the rural panel and the college corporation, and the college principal is also a member.

The rural panel, in consultation with the college, decided to commission detailed, industry-specific LMI. The TEC funded specific research and a project officer to undertake research locally and within the college. The only cost to the college was the involvement of time to guide the research, which made this a cost-effective way of identifying new information.

The output of the initial project will be detailed LMI on the size, age profile and adequacy of the labour market in agriculture. The next stage will be for the TEC and college to develop a joint strategy to deliver the required education and training.

Student tracking and student survey information

3.11   Student tracking information can be captured and stored on:

- enquiries
- applications
- initial enrolments
- retention at census points during the course
- qualification outcomes
- initial and long-term destinations.

3.12   Tracking information can be used for:

- analysis of why prospective students did not enrol, and chasing non-enrollers
- investigation of enrolments of particular target groups

- curriculum team analysis of recruitment, retention and achievement, and chasing potential non-completers

- evaluation of promotional activities

- analysis of success in converting enquiries to enrolments to completions.

Student surveys also contribute important information which can be used as part of the marketing intelligence picture.

Student tracking

A group of colleges worked with FEDA, funded by the FEFC, to develop an integrated approach to student tracking. The project specifies the student tracking information colleges are likely to need, how they can obtain it, and what systems are required to capture, analyse and report it. More details can be found in *Student Tracking* **(Donovan, 1996).**

Using qualitative market intelligence

3.13   Valuable information can be gleaned from the local and national media, from personal contacts between college staff and the local community, and from the range of professional inservice and updating activities in which staff engage. All colleges gather this kind of marketing intelligence. To make best use of it, however, requires a systematic processing of information-gathering and analysis — and one which genuinely informs decision-making. It therefore needs to be timely and focused.

3.14   Although this type of data is relatively 'soft' when compared with more quantitative evidence obtained through desk and primary research, it is often more up to date and specific to local circumstances. News of proposed housing developments, expansion by local businesses or initiatives by voluntary agencies will often be reported in the local media long before they appear in official forecasts or statistics.

3.15   This has some interesting potential applications in the world of further education. A case study serves to show how local press information can be used.

Meeting new business leaders

The marketing manager of a West Midlands college regularly scanned the local press and the chamber of commerce newsletter for items concerning newly appointed senior managers who were joining companies in the area. She would write letters of congratulation to them, and offer to discuss with them ways in which the college might be of service in the future. This low-cost and straightforward technique enabled the college to obtain successful openings in a number of companies with which it had not formerly done business.

Analysis of other providers

3.16 Successful colleges also gather information about the plans and activities of other providers. This entails, for example, looking at:

- range

- quality

- recent changes in curriculum development

- new and discontinued courses

- achievement

- trends in publicity and recruitment

- inspection outcomes

- financial results

- performance indicators

- staffing.

3.17 Analysis needs to be systematic and allow for effective comparison across the spectrum of other provision and against the college's position. Even when the relationship between neighbouring institutions is collaborative, it is still important to have independent sources of information about what other organisations are doing.

Building a database on other providers

 **The marketing team at one college has built a database from staff and student information on other local providers. This draws on: information from staff gleaned from contacts with schools and colleges about their curriculum activities and plans; information from enrolled students about their feeder schools and other providers they had considered; and limited information gained from the systematic follow-up of enquiries that had not turned into enrolments. The database is used to support programme decisions and to brief members of staff before meetings with partner institutions and other providers.**

Effective market research

3.18 In marketing contexts outside education, market research covers the range of activities necessary to gather and analyse data in order to inform decisions about the marketing mix. Successful organisations will usually make a significant investment in research since an increased understanding of the nature of intended markets is seen as essential to the development of effective marketing strategies. Market research is normally conducted in order to:

- **forecast demand** for the efficient allocation of resources

- **identify market wants, needs, opportunities, and attitudes** to design and deliver the right services, to develop a positive identity and to communicate persuasively with customers, funders and opinion formers

- **evaluate provision and performance** in order to review and develop services and to reassess corporate objectives and strategies.

3.19 Colleges seeking to maximise the impact of market research should:

- ensure that customer surveys are timely, regular and capable of providing information which can genuinely influence decisions about future college programmes, the marketing mix and service provision

- tap the opinions of non-users of the college's services: why prospective entrants from schools choose to go elsewhere, for example, and what might be done to make possible enrolments more secure. It is also essential to establish accurately why certain enrolled students subsequently withdraw from courses

- make sure that the brief for any commissioned research is clear, precise and realistic. In particular:

  — identify the key decisions the research is intended to address

  — specify the format for the contents and presentation of the final research report

  — specify the analysis necessary to provide this information

  — determine the kind of data that must be assembled to carry out these analyses

  — design instruments and a sampling plan for required data that will be collected by the college

- gather data on those key factors with the potential for influencing customer choice:

  — demographic and factual factors (sex, ethnicity, social class, previous qualifications)

  — attitudinal factors, such as customer perceptions of programme choice, convenience, quality of teaching and guidance, facilities

- establish mechanisms for gathering qualitative data:

  — feedback from student representatives on course boards

  — complaints procedure

  — structured interviews by phone or in person, using a set agenda

  — focus groups of between eight and 12 members of a target group, using a set interview and discussion schedule and led by an experienced facilitator

—   questionnaires that allow comparison, for example, between groups, or which seek responses from target groups.

Allocating an appropriate budget

3.20   The NAO found that marketing expenditure varied from 1 per cent to almost 3 per cent of total expenditure in the colleges they visited (NAO, 1997a).   There was striking variation in the amount each college spent to recruit additional students, from around £30 a head to almost £140 a head.   The most likely problem is that too much money is directed towards general promotional materials and insufficient resources are devoted to the key data on which the marketing strategy depends.   Any research needs to work towards a clearly defined brief in which the costs and benefits are made explicit.   In judging the level of investment required, it is worth weighing in the balance the likely costs of misinformed or unwise strategic decisions, such as the development and promotion of a course for which the customer base is insignificant or non-existent.

CHECKLIST

This checklist is intended to assist with the review and action planning process.

		Yes	No	Action needed
a.	Is there effective and readily available external data, including for example population information, employer databases, school-leaver information and database marketing?	☐	☐	☐
b.	Is the college working with the TEC to generate specific LMI which is useful to the college?	☐	☐	☐
c.	Does the college use student tracking data, student feedback and TEC LMI to inform the marketing strategy?	☐	☐	☐
d.	Is the information system integrated rather than disparate?	☐	☐	☐
e.	Do research data inform operational and strategic decisions?	☐	☐	☐
f.	Are staff contacts gathered and used?	☐	☐	☐
g.	Are informal sources such as the local media monitored?	☐	☐	☐
h.	Are customer surveys and surveys of non-users conducted regularly?	☐	☐	☐
i.	Are briefs for commissioned research clear, precise and realistic?	☐	☐	☐
j.	Are qualitative and quantitative data both used?	☐	☐	☐
k.	What proportion of the marketing budget is spent on promotion as opposed to research?	☐	☐	☐
l.	Is a cost-benefit analysis carried out on market research activities?	☐	☐	☐

Chapter 4

Market Segmentation

Introduction

4.1   Market segmentation is the process of dividing the overall potential market. These divisions, known as segments, comprise different potential targets, each of which shares certain characteristics. Typically colleges recognise and plan for the following segments:

- 16 to 19 year olds aiming to progress to higher education or to enter the labour market

- young unemployed people seeking a route into work

- unemployed adults anxious to return to the labour market

- women returners

- employers requiring training for their workforces or other services such as consultancy

- people wishing to improve or update their existing skills and qualifications

- the community, including voluntary groups and individuals seeking leisure activities

- people with learning difficulties and/or disabilities.

The purpose of segmentation is to establish the best alignment between what the college offers and what its customers require.

Policy Considerations

4.2   The following key issues need to be taken into consideration.

- work on producing accurate and appropriate segmentation which has neither too narrow nor too broad a focus for each segment

- establish good measures of market share and trends within each segment

- differentiate the strategies and customise services for each segment.

Guidance

How Specific Should Market Segments Be?

4.3   In one sense, the ultimate segment is each individual student, since all students come with different aspirations, attitudes and requirements. In practical terms, a broader strategy is required. The college in the following case study adopted a course of action that would allow for individual tastes and requirements.

Helping learners access the right course for them

 **CASE STUDY** **A college in the South East is heavily involved in non-vocational adult education. This provision is presented as a 'seamless robe' — potential students looking for part-time provision can choose from a variety of courses which are identified by subject rather than by accreditation, status or funding source. Anyone interested in a particular topic can look at a brochure which lists everything on offer, from full-cost one-day courses through LEA-supported 10-week non-accredited courses to FEFC-funded 36-week accredited courses. This allows potential students to be aware of a ladder of opportunity and progression which encourages participation.**

4.4   While broad brush segmentation has its undoubted uses, in practice, more specific segmentation is necessary if a college is to be fully responsive to the nuances of the market (or markets) it intends to serve. Colleges with the most convincing records in terms of growth, retention and achievement tend to extend the concept of segmentation with a view to addressing the full range of different needs. They are aware of the pitfalls of compiling categories that are too broad which may make individuals feel they are being treated with an insensitive uniformity. Avoiding this danger means:

- looking to target a specific group within a broad category

- recognising when different approaches in the various segments are required

- being aware of sections of the community whose interests may be overlooked in a broad brush strategy

- distinguishing between large companies and small- to medium-sized enterprises (SMEs) when focusing on the employer market

- including funders and other influences within identified segments, including:

  - parents

  - employers (including those who employ current students)

  - TECs

  - government agencies

  - voluntary organisations

  - elected representatives

  - the media.

The following three case studies show approaches to segmentation which tackle potential problems in applying a segmentation strategy.

Segments for competition against specialists

 A college's local art and design provision operates alongside specialist regional providers whose image is promoted through high-quality, well-focused brochures. To rely on the promotion of the college's own art and design offering using the college prospectus aimed at a wider segment would concede much of the market to the specialist provider. A concentrated 'subsegment' focus is required. The college responded by producing its own specialist publicity material which it sends directly to the equivalent specialists in schools, and runs regular studio sessions to bring prospective students into the college.

Segmentation to meet the challenge from school sixth forms

 Colleges operating alongside well-established school sixth forms have responded by packaging the marketing of GCE A level and GNVQ provision separately from other 16–19 provision. In this way, they have enhanced their ability to demonstrate the quality and variety of their A level and GNVQ curriculum offer. One college, faced with a reduction in its general GNVQ business course, met the challenge by developing a niche in GNVQ business with a distinctive journalism component.

Distinctive needs within each segment

 A number of colleges have identified and responded to the distinct needs of those within their community approaching retirement age, and have provided courses specific to their needs and interests. One of the keys to this seems to be making it clear to these prospective learners that they will not be grouped with 16 year olds, but will be able to learn (and enjoy themselves) in an adult environment.

Measures of Market Share and Trends

4.5   Most colleges have a fair grasp of their proportion of the school-leavers' market. It is, after all, the easiest to measure. Measuring share elsewhere is more difficult, but worth the effort. Trends in market share over time are as important as the precise nature of the existing share. Key lessons in this are:

- it is wasteful to devote resources to sustain provision which attracts only a narrow share of a limited market

- using enrolment figures as the main performance indicator is not enough, since it is quite possible to increase enrolments in an expanding market and yet still to lose the overall share to other providers

- significant shifts in market share do not take place rapidly, unless a radical shift to the marketing mix leads to new and substantial competitive advantage

- consideration of market share and segmentation needs to include an awareness of the equal opportunity needs of specific groups

- it is wise to recognise the existence of wider generic markets when seeking to boost market share in some segments. For example, colleges which offer community-based leisure activities immediately step into the territory occupied by the leisure industry

- it is helpful to distinguish between market participation (the proportion of the market in education and training) and market penetration (the proportion of the market which attends the college in question rather than all providers). *Identifying and Addressing Needs* (IES, 1997) has a helpful section on this distinction, and its uses in segmentation.

Customised Provision

4.6   Once sensible segments have been identified, these can be characterised according to the markets and services involved to develop appropriate marketing approaches for each segment. For example, a questionnaire analysis of the existing student body can be used to identify the profile of students who are significantly dissatisfied with their college experience. The analysis may reveal that such students share a distinct demographic and attitudinal profile. Their problems can be tackled using targeted action such as counselling and mentoring which it might not be economical to pursue for all students.

4.7   Factors which contribute to the customisation of college services to meet identified needs include:

- the successful implementation of individual learning programmes

- effective tutorial support systems

- proactive student support units sharing links with the curriculum and marketing plans

- the use of computer-based techniques.

The following two case studies show colleges using innovative methods to tailor their services to suit the requirements of particular groups.

Identifying individual learning activities

The recording of student transactions using electronic swipe cards is a valuable application of technology. A number of colleges have now issued students with an identity card for security purposes, and some of these now operate as swipe cards too. They can be used to buy things in the refectory and to borrow books and other materials from the library. In some colleges in the United States, this technology extends to making it possible for students to obtain a computerised update on course progress using the card, and even in some cases to change their option choices using the card. Such a database provides a valuable source of evidence of individual service use, which can be used to inform the future pattern of provision.

Targeting basic skills support

A college in South Wales identified as a strategic objective the need to tackle barriers to learning caused by poor basic skills. In order to fulfil this objective, a new school of learning support was established at one of the college sites to make sure that a consistent, high-quality service operates across all its learning support workshops. All first-year full-time vocational students received an hour of basic skills support each week in communications, maths and IT. Students' communication skills were screened, results returned to course tutors and any students identified as needing extra support were given counselling to attend drop-in centres. The drop-in centres were open for 27 hours a week, day and evening, and were open to all students as well as people in the local community. The communications workshop operated an outreach programme where students used laptops to gain basic skills and IT accreditation. The new school worked with the Centre for Art and Design Technology to create a bank of multimedia resources to meet students' basic skills needs. In conjunction with the School of Vocational Access, the school has established a team to assess and support mainstream students with learning difficulties.

CHECKLIST This checklist is intended to assist with the review and action planning process.

		Yes	No	Action needed
a.	Does the college recognise other providers within each niche, as well as overall?	☐	☐	☐
b.	Is enough done to define the needs of each segment?	☐	☐	☐
c.	Are subsegments (for example, adults approaching retirement) identified where appropriate?	☐	☐	☐
d.	Is the employer market segmented as well as the individual market?	☐	☐	☐
e.	Have funders and influences within each segment been identified?	☐	☐	☐
f.	Are resources wastefully devoted to provision which attracts only a limited share of a declining market?	☐	☐	☐
g.	Are enrolment figures supplemented by market share information as a performance indicator?	☐	☐	☐
h.	Are significant shifts in market share recorded efficiently?	☐	☐	☐
i.	Is the college's understanding of the equal opportunity needs of specific groups satisfactory?	☐	☐	☐
j.	Does the adopted method of segmentation recognise when college niche providers are competing with other generic providers?	☐	☐	☐
k.	Does the college offer individualised learning programmes?	☐	☐	☐
l.	Are tutorial support systems well targeted?	☐	☐	☐
m.	Are student support systems linked to the curriculum and marketing?	☐	☐	☐
n.	Is the college's use of IT effective?	☐	☐	☐

Chapter 5

Curriculum Development and Quality Assurance

Introduction

5.1   The thread between curriculum, quality and customer satisfaction is fundamental to the process by which a college seeks to embed itself as the major provider in its natural marketplace. The curriculum is the core business of the college, and if that core is flawed, incomplete or unwanted, the rest of the college's activities, including marketing, are undermined. Hence the focus on the curriculum throughout this guide.

Policy Considerations

5.2   The following key issues need to be taken into consideration.

- when examining the curriculum portfolio, colleges should inject a market perspective into the process of curriculum review and development

- use quality assurance processes and quality improvement projects to contribute to marketing

- integrate the approach to marketing, curriculum planning and quality assurance.

Guidance

Market-led Curriculum Review and Development

5.3   New product development tends to be considered by those outside education as the most important element of the marketing function, rather than publicity and PR. In the most successful colleges, great attention is paid to the development of clear priorities and realistic market-led strategies and, as part of that, a planned process of curriculum investment and divestment; that is, the introduction of new courses and the closure of old ones. Financial realities have encouraged many colleges to take a radical look at their future needs. The consequences have been:

- scrutiny of enrolments. In many cases, the 80–20 rule applies: fewer than 20 per cent of courses provide 80 per cent of the enrolments. The logical consequence is more realistic portfolio management, without losing the minority markets which are important in the light of the college's overall mission

- a focus on programme budgeting as an integral part of the curriculum, not as an afterthought

- more astute anticipation of trends and building that into resource deployment

- flexibility in staff appointments, such as specific and short-term contracts

- the incorporation of flexibility into building developments to accommodate changing patterns of demand.

Reviewing the curriculum portfolio

 **One college, faced with the decline of its full-time programmes in construction, undertook a radical review of the curriculum in order to offer more flexibility. Because many of their target students were working shifts, they opened a flexible learning centre covering all the construction trades which was open for evening and weekend business. They used specialist staff to develop learning modules in their own trades, and carried out staff development to 'multi-skill' staff for delivery of any of the modules. The result was a turn-round in the recruitment decline.**

5.4   The enthusiasm of grassroots staff for new developments in their programme area is part of the lifeblood of colleges. But course teams need to operate within a structure of curriculum review and development which requires justification in business terms. This is where co-operative and constructive relationships between curriculum teams and marketing staff has its greatest effect. A business-oriented decision to introduce a new course or withdraw an old one needs to be informed by:

- historical student numbers, costs and income

- prospective student numbers in the short-, medium- and long-term

- activities and plans of other providers

- prospective funding sources

- projected costs and resource implications

- short-term costs associated with start-up or withdrawal

- how the programme fits into the college's portfolio

- how its introduction or withdrawal would affect the image of the college.

5.5   In other words, a proper cost benefit analysis of the proposal is needed. Many of the factors mentioned are marketing as well as financial issues.

5.6   To be effective, curriculum development needs to form an integral part of the college marketing plan. There should be regular reviews of curriculum provision in terms of its opportunity cost; that is, the cost of maintaining any course or other service measured in terms of the alternative uses for the resources allocated. This requires longer-term thinking. The short-term avoidable costs arising from the withdrawal of provision are often minimal since staff, and sometimes accommodation, can usually be reallocated for use in other programme areas.

5.7   At senior management level, the major decisions are concerned with investment and divestment across whole areas of the curriculum. Major savings and opportunities for the reallocation of resources are more likely to come from the withdrawal of whole areas of the curriculum, particularly those that are capital intensive. This kind of divestment decision has major implications for a college's relationship with its community, and should not be taken in isolation from the strategic plan or without informing and consulting the FEFC. Nonetheless, major realignments of the curriculum may be necessary if resources are to be freed up from areas of decline in order to support the levels of investment that can bring major returns — especially in areas in which responsiveness to demand has been constrained due to lack of resources.

Dealing with declining markets

 **In one college in Yorkshire, the curriculum review uncovered a common problem: the college's construction provision was in decline and represented a drain on resources. The college mission committed the college to retaining the curriculum area, so a major effort was devoted to marketing the programme area in order to increase student numbers, reviewing the curriculum delivery to make it more accessible and cost-effective, and to attracting alternative sources of funding. Two years later, although the construction area is still subsidised, its financial position is stable and the college can afford to keep it in the portfolio.**

5.8   At department and section level, curriculum innovation can be carried through rapidly and flexibly. In the short-course market aimed at corporate clients, and in non-vocational education, the most successful colleges are constantly adapting provision to meet current needs in response to new legislation, economic trends or simply fashion. Course contents can be repackaged or titles changed in order to sustain their appeal or in response to new market opportunities.

Making Quality Assurance Contribute to Effective Marketing

5.9   A number of colleges have developed effective systems of self-assessment, enabling them to examine the curriculum, its delivery and support services with the active involvement of course teams, students and external stakeholders. This approach informs the basis of the FEFC's approach to inspection from 1997-98 and will be the foundation for the development of moves towards accreditation. Contrary to popular impressions, much effective marketing activity in the world beyond education is concerned with the review of the marketing mix and minor adjustments which will maintain and improve the quality of service. This approach also characterises colleges which display an ethos of continual improvement at all levels.

5.10 To gain full benefits from quality assurance, it is useful to:

- ensure that course teams are directly involved in the review process, since this minimises staff sensitivities about negative feedback

- engage all staff, teaching and non-teaching, in the task of giving the needs of customers precedence

- heed the evidence on the reasons for student withdrawals emerging from the process of the review and provide strong systems to combat those concerns, for example, by providing student mentoring systems to help 'at risk' students cope with college life.

Retention action

 A college on Merseyside has developed an extremely successful range of strategies to improve student retention. In 1992, almost a quarter of its students were not completing their programmes of study. It was estimated that the college was losing over £1 million a year in funding as a result of the high levels of student drop-out. Retention action teams (RATs) were established in response, and involved large numbers of staff. All full-time lecturers were asked to consider the retention issue in relation to their particular curriculum area and to identify and develop a task or project to improve the situation. They were encouraged to work in teams of two or three. Some part-time lecturers and assistant principals were also involved. Almost 60 projects were developed and included marketing activities such as:

- student perception surveys carried out by students as part of their course

- synchronising enhanced curriculum activities with times of high withdrawal

- introduction of a termly student forum

- integration of careers input into the curriculum

- introduction of a student newsletter

- identification of students most at risk from early withdrawal

- poster displays of guidelines on improving retention around the college.

The college has now achieved an overall retention rate in excess of 82 per cent. Not only are fewer students withdrawing from their courses, but withdrawals are occurring later. The college estimates that the increase in student completion has generated approximately £200,000 of additional income a year. The college is continuing to pursue these strategies in order to improve retention rates to over 85 per cent.

Charters

5.11   The *Charter for Further Education* has been a stimulus to a number of colleges to communicate the college's quality standards to their students and other clients. The terms of their funding agreements with the FEFC require colleges to have charters. Connected with these developments has been an increasing attention paid to complaints and grievance procedures, to ensure that there is appropriate redress for dissatisfied students, and that justifiable complaints are seen to be dealt with.

5.12   More broadly, the approach which lies behind the introduction of college charters, that of seeking out and acting on customer feedback, is one of the cornerstones of effective marketing. College quality systems that include analysis of feedback from students, employers and other clients, and which are linked to the marketing and curriculum planning cycles to pick up action points, put this into practice.

5.13   Many colleges supplement such elements with a student handbook setting out advice, guidance and entitlements. Some successfully involve students working with course teams on the process of review and development.

Achieving an Integrated Approach

5.14   Perhaps the most compelling finding in the fieldwork contributing to this guide was the importance of close co-ordination between market research, curriculum development, student services, quality assurance, publicity and PR. Where this co-ordination was lacking, clear tensions arose which inhibited the effectiveness of corporate marketing. Where there were no 'them and us' attitudes, and all these activities were effectively integrated, the benefits to colleges appeared to be considerable.

5.15   As described later in chapter 7, no single organisational structure provides a ready solution; the key is a pervasive ethos which places a high value on flexible and collaborative working. The following case study shows how a wide range of services can make an effective contribution if managed alongside the marketing function.

Achieving integration through the management structure

CASE STUDY

A South East college has a mission which commits it to encouraging the widest possible participation by all the people who live in its catchment area. This commitment is supported by an extensive range of services which it offers alongside the more conventional marketing activities. As well as making a significant investment in high-quality promotional materials, the college has also established information and guidance centres, student support services and a range of learner support services. By operating these services centrally under the same line management as the marketing department, there is a sense of co-ordination and co-operation between the range of services on offer which ensures that once people have been attracted to the college, they have access to

information and guidance. **This promotes the college's programmes where appropriate but also acts professionally to direct individuals towards other providers if they can meet the need better. Links with curriculum teams are strong to ensure a smooth handover of students to their chosen programme teams. This coherent package of services has enabled the college to make its mission statement a reality and widen participation considerably.**

5.16   Effective integration is characterised by the active involvement of marketing personnel in supplying marketing intelligence and research information to course teams, and in discussing with them the implications for course review and development. At the same time, a positive relationship between curriculum and marketing staff in the development of an active and responsive programme of publicity and PR is mutually beneficial.

CHECKLIST

This checklist is intended to assist with the review and action planning process.

		Yes	No	Action needed
a.	Are curriculum investment and divestment based on market needs, enrolment and retention trends, and financial realities?	☐	☐	☐
b.	Does the college have a genuinely flexible curriculum, supported by staffing and accommodation?	☐	☐	☐
c.	In curriculum review, is the opportunity cost of courses needing subsidy analysed?	☐	☐	☐
d.	Does the college undertake continual improvement of details of the marketing mix based on self-assessment findings?	☐	☐	☐
e.	Are course teams involved in curriculum review as well as just course review?	☐	☐	☐
f.	Are students involved in curriculum review?	☐	☐	☐
g.	Are market research, curriculum development, student services, quality assurance, publicity and public relations integrated?	☐	☐	☐
h.	Are there close working relationships between course teams and marketing staff?	☐	☐	☐

Chapter 6

Selling, Publicity and Customer Relations

Introduction

6.1   A finely tuned curriculum and high-quality delivery count for nothing if the 'product' remains unsold. A key task for colleges is to ensure that customers are sufficiently persuaded by the services on offer to buy them. This is not something which can be left to chance: colleges need to be both systematic and innovative in how they sell, and to place the emphasis on strategies which will give the best chance of retaining customers over time. That can best be achieved by working in partnership with customers wherever possible.

6.2   Selling activities should be supported by efficient communication with the markets a college aims to serve. Not to do so is fraught with risk: when compared with other sectors, there is evidence that the college sector has, at least until recently, suffered from a poorer and less well-defined public image. Compared with school sixth forms and universities, further education colleges generally have to work harder to get the message across.

Policy Considerations

6.3   The following key issues need to be taken into consideration.

- develop comprehensive guidance on selling within a selling plan so that it can be used as a framework for all the college's selling and promotion

- have a coherent approach to promotion, based on a few clear, repeated messages about benefits

- produce attractive and effective PR materials, with differentiation for niche services and different customer groups

- use appropriate selling techniques to get the message across

- develop partnerships with the college's customers: a 'relationship marketing' approach.

Guidance

The Selling Plan

6.4   The approach to selling in the college should be made explicit in a plan which includes guidance to which all staff have access. It should determine:

- strategies for extending customer relationships and encouraging repeat business

- an effective system for logging and pursuing leads, either 'hot' or 'cold'

- who in the college leads on sales, and whether there should be a designated salesforce

- how the benefits of networking are to be maximised

- the scope, costs and benefits of any externally commissioned activity

- what customer information is to be stored and how it can be most readily accessed

- the resources to support the plan, and the means by which they can be accessed.

Promoting the College

6.5   Potential students and corporate clients face a barrage of promotional messages every day. It is a mistake to assume that what is transmitted will be received. If sales communications are to be successful, they must be:

- **sustained**   promotional activities should be continual: messages and images must be repeated constantly, and regularly revived, if they are to be absorbed

- **appealing**   messages and images, and the media by which they are communicated, need to be selected to have the maximum appeal

- **targeted**   messages aimed at particular client groups are generally more effective than those using a 'scattergun' approach.

6.6   The selection of media and images to appeal to targeted audiences is especially important. Messages and images need to concentrate on the factors which 'hook' the audiences the college is trying to attract. These messages, therefore, will be related to the benefits and outcomes resulting from education and training, rather than, say, detailed course descriptions or factual accounts of college services. For most people, course structures and regulations are a means to the end, and successful colleges do not allow the small print about provision to obscure key messages concerning the benefits.

6.7   The more images, messages and media are tailored to the requirements of a specific audience, the more likely the message is to strike home. It is rare for one message or image to appeal with equal success to different client groups. Although separately targeted publicity is more costly, it is usually far more effective. Colleges can aim messages and images within the same brochure at different segments rather than attempting a lowest common denominator of appeal throughout.

Creating PR materials

6.8 The criteria for effective PR materials are:

- an attractive and readily identifiable visual identity

- 'substance' behind the image

- scope for adaptation according to circumstances within an overall corporate framework

- an effective and attractive appearance that transfers well to other media — for example, in different sizes, or black and white reproduction

- relevance to specific niche services — specialist art and design provision, for example — by the development of distinctive brand identities. This can be achieved without the loss of the overall image by unobtrusive application of the corporate identity as part of the brand definition.

6.9 Most people associate the college marketing strategy with its prospectus, and in many colleges, it is the most expensive element in the marketing budget. Moreover, it is the aspect of marketing where most specialist staff in colleges are employed. However, it may not be the most effective means of reaching the target audiences.

6.10 Instead, there is merit in giving thought to what might be the most productive form of sales literature, in particular when addressing market niches. An approach which differentiates the constituent parts, targeting materials within a corporate image, rather than relying on a general prospectus may well be more effective.

6.11 For this reason, many colleges have ceased or reduced their production of a single prospectus and have moved instead to producing a combination of targeted leaflets and brochures for particular groups. For example, a college might produce two separate brochures for full- and part-time programmes, and a third to support sales to corporate customers, supplemented by short leaflets on each particular programme or groups of programmes on offer.

6.12 Another effective way of getting the message across is by publishing a college tabloid, promoting courses indirectly by telling success stories of current students. This taps into the research on the importance of word of mouth, and is more likely to be read than a prospectus by all but the most dedicated prospective student. Some colleges without the in-house skills to produce newspapers are collaborating successfully with their local daily or weekly papers to produce and deliver special editions or inserts. The important thing is to make sure that the publicity material is accessible to prospective customers.

6.13 General research findings indicate that magazine advertising has the most impact on purchasers of general goods and services (29 per cent). Word of mouth is also highly placed (23 per cent) while radio advertising and direct phone calls are considered the least successful (4 per cent). In colleges, surveys have shown that word of mouth is the key influence.

Reinforcing the message

CASE STUDY

One college's methods of selling include:

- **internal posters for existing students**
- **a diary and student guide**
- **an internal newsletter**
- **a loyalty scheme associated with a magazine**
- **a poster for schools**
- **a city centre leaflet campaign**
- **bus advertising**
- **street banners**
- **advertisements in local cinemas**
- **a college-specific careers guide**
- **a World Wide Web site;**
- **cards to school students sent out to coincide with GCSE results.**

6.14   Underlying the whole approach, however, is the need to target each segment — post-16, employers, adult returners — in a way which is alert to the nuances of each. The main approaches available are:

- direct mail
- advertising
- the press
- telemarketing
- presentations and exhibitions.

Direct mail

6.15   Direct mail is most effective when its recipients are carefully targeted; blanket coverage can be an expensive indulgence. It needs to be tailored to the individual customer's needs and interests, rather than being an alternative form of conventional advertising. Mailshots require an accurate and appropriate database to avoid annoyance to potential recruits, or expensive mistakes.

6.16   Direct mail is significantly more effective in some areas than in others. General research findings indicate that, while 19 per cent of direct mail campaigns in the food sector are successful in sales terms, the figure is much lower in business services, while for exhibitions and courses the figure is only 8 per cent. In gauging the level of effort and investment to devote to any direct mail enterprise, it is helpful to identify the level of business anticipated as a consequence of the initiative, and to monitor progress against that target.

Advertising

6.17   In taking advertising space, it is important to:

- place the advertisement where prospective customers are likely to see it

- balance the cost of advertising against the number of enquiries and enrolments arising

- maintain a detailed log of past expenditure on advertising and its outcomes

- identify clearly what is being sold, and project a consistent image of the college.

6.18   Research evidence indicates that new products gain greater benefits from media advertising than established products.

The press

6.19   Successful colleges exploit the value of adroitly placed newsworthy stories, rather than incurring an undue amount of expenditure on advertising. The next case study typifies how some colleges have an eye for positive media coverage.

Positive press coverage

The local media are always interested in 'people' stories — and colleges are full of them. One college got its name and a picture in the local daily paper in a feature about its oldest student recruit, a grandmother who had taken up a course there. Another college contracted a PR firm and introduced a 'suggestion form' for staff to alert the firm to possible news stories. Thirty-seven such stories appeared in the first year. Another specialist college spends very little on advertising, but generates press stories from teaching and learning achievements, so creating recognition for students as well as positive coverage for the college. For example, the college's bakery section achieved local and national publicity for its entry in *The Guinness Book of Records* for baking the largest ever loaf.

Telemarketing

6.20   The key factors in the use of the telephone — telemarketing — in effective selling are:

- consistency of approach across the organisation, and one which aims to be as personal and individual as possible

- accurate and up-to-date customer details

- a phone system and staffing levels which can cope with incoming enquiries in a professional, positive manner.

6.21   It is also important to monitor and evaluate the effectiveness of telephone selling; the relationship, for example, between numbers dialled, calls made and sales achieved. When assessing the effectiveness of this method, overheads need to be taken into account. These include staff, equipment and training. A recent analysis of telemarketing suggests that the average cost per phone call varies from between £5 and £10 for incoming calls and from £5 to £15 for outgoing calls.

6.22 A centralised telemarketing unit can ensure a much more consumer-oriented approach and a stronger likelihood of converting enquiries to enrolments.

Presentations and exhibitions

6.23 To make effective presentations and exhibitions, it is important to:

- ensure that careful records are kept of contacts made

- follow up such contacts systematically

- ensure that each individual's networking contacts are shared

- devise a means of judging whether exhibition expenditure is providing value for money

- ensure that the context is one in which those attending are genuinely potential customers

- consider the use of exhibitions specially to launch new products — something which is common outside education and training.

Customer Partnerships and Relationship Marketing

6.24 Heavy expenditure on publicity and advertising does not guarantee an upsurge in recruitment or client enthusiasm. An alternative, frequently found in successful colleges in the FEDA–KPMG study, is 'relationship marketing'. Relationship marketing is the nurturing of mutually beneficial contacts with target audiences and the development of supportive networks. This approach recognises the enormous importance to service organisations of word of mouth, direct contact, with actual and potential customers.

Industry lunches

 **A valuable yet low-cost approach to partnership by one specialist agriculture college has been its industry lunches. As part of a capital appeal, the principal launched a programme of lunches for senior individuals in the industry and the local community. The lunches were low-key affairs in terms of organisation and expenditure and used the college refectory with table service. Each lunch was followed by a brief tour of college facilities and informal presentations. The benefits have been significant. The appeal has raised some £480,000 to date, and college puts much of the success down to the personal commitment generated at the lunches.**

6.25 The mark of a successful client–provider relationship is where the former asks the latter for more. It is much easier to sell to a convinced and trusting existing customer.

Evidence from outside the world of education suggests that it costs between three and seven times more to recruit new customers than to retain existing ones. There is really no substitute for established relationships, and these need to be fostered and maintained with care. The aim must be to establish a partnership with each customer in a way which will encourage each one to view the college as a reliable source of support. Two factors which contribute to this are: first, a recognition that customer partnerships will vary depending on the characteristics of the market segment, and second, the necessity for a holistic approach, and 'mind set'. This is not something which can be left to senior management aspiration, but needs to be part of the college ethos.

6.26 Four areas in which of relationship marketing is likely to succeed are:

- media relations

- liaison with schools

- involvement in the community

- liaison with employers.

Media relations

6.27 Marketing teams can make the stimulation of positive news in the published media a priority. The aim is to encourage editorial copy rather than paid-for advertising, the generation of positive newsworthy stories and the establishment of a close professional relationship with the staff of local newspapers and radio stations. Senior managers are particularly valuable as ambassadors for the college, coming into contact as they do with influential opinion-formers in the community. There is value, too, in establishing effective mechanisms for trawling curriculum teams and support staff for potentially newsworthy stories, thus providing the college with opportunities to communicate positive messages about its own successes. Programmes of forward events, such as student involvement in national competitions or charitable activities, can also be used to promote the college.

Liaison with schools

6.28 All colleges maintain some form of contact with local schools. Such contacts are most successful where there is a coherent plan based on a careful analysis of the progression routes of school-leavers at 16. This helps to inform programmes of contact which can sustain good relations with those schools where there are mutual benefits in such contact.

6.29 Colleges typically take up the opportunities available to them to contribute to careers evenings for year-11 pupils and their parents, and to supply relevant information, including the distribution of prospectuses and other course literature. Schools are required to provide access to information concerning the range of courses at 16-plus. In some cases, effective local partnerships between colleges and schools have been established. In others, collaborative approaches are less common.

6.30 Colleges can be proactive in making direct contact with school pupils and their parents, and with other potential audiences by mounting their own careers evenings and open days, advertised in the local press, on posters and through mailshots. These events have the attraction of being under the control of the college and on college premises. They can be professionally designed and mounted to show the college in the best possible light. A number of colleges successfully follow up this direct contact by mounting 'taster' days so that prospective students have a chance to sample something of the reality of college life. Current students who previously attended schools in the area are often the most effective and persuasive advocates for the college amongst their peer group. The impact on any wider partnerships with schools must, however, be considered.

6.31 Alternatively, innovative approaches in relationship marketing with schools are being seen in colleges wishing to escape an ethos of costly and unproductive competition. Typically these approaches involve staff and pupils (including those from lower and middle schools) having access to college facilities. Some colleges have even extended this approach to involve primary schools. This helps create a climate in which progression to college is a natural step for those students for whom it offers the most appropriate programmes and learning environment.

Involvement in the community

6.32 Awareness of the college in the community is enhanced when marketing and curriculum staff are involved with local voluntary groups and organisations. Offers of help and assistance by the college, and access to college facilities, are again ways of developing personal relationships with individuals in the community who can then become advocates for the college.

Liaison with employers

6.33 Contact with corporate clients is often managed separately from school and community liaison, often under the auspices of a business services unit. Successful colleges usually work to a planned programme of employer contacts, aimed at retaining existing clients and targeting prospective additions.

6.34 Liaison with curriculum teams is also important here. Where existing clients are concerned, research evidence suggests that the main source of dissatisfaction is inadequate feedback on the progress of employees on college training programmes. Efficient reporting mechanisms therefore need to be established and maintained. Colleges can also profitably draw on the technical expertise of curriculum teams when the discussion of services with a potential client requires a level of detail or expertise beyond that possessed by sales staff. In the case of collaborative provision (CP) arrangements, a number of colleges have found it sensible to allocate staff for maintaining contact and ensuring effective quality assurance.

6.35 The maintenance of effective contacts with the local TEC is also a necessary feature of promotion in the corporate market. The TEC is usually a major client in its own right, and personal contacts with key personnel need to be developed and maintained. Colleges have also sought to establish relationships with employers outside the context of direct selling and negotiation through their involvement in local networks such as business clubs and chambers of commerce, and by holding events specifically targeted at employers. A number of colleges have in the past successfully involved employers in breakfast briefings and in events such as joint careers exhibitions.

6.36 The importance of repeat business from existing satisfied customers as a key aspect of marketing has already been highlighted in this guide, and this is a vital area in which the relationship marketing approach can pay dividends.

Relationship marketing to retain existing customers

CASE STUDY

One college's policy for retaining existing students and corporate customers includes the following:

- **low key, regular and well-targeted publicity events for long-term customers, including breakfast briefings and links between senior staff and key corporate clients with whom they are expected to build and maintain relationships**

- **fast response times and a sense of 'preferential treatment' for key customers**

- **drawing in key customers (including student groups) to PR activities of mutual benefit**

- **efficient exchange of relevant customer information throughout college departments, using an up-to-date marketing database.**

CHECKLIST   **This checklist is intended to assist with the review and action planning process.**

		Yes	No	Action needed
a.	Is there a selling plan to provide a framework for all selling and promotion?	☐	☐	☐
b.	Does the plan contain explicit strategies for developing customer relationships?	☐	☐	☐
c.	Is there an effective system for storing and accessing customer information and capturing leads?	☐	☐	☐
d.	Is there clear staff responsibility for sales?	☐	☐	☐
e.	Is all internally and externally commissioned work subject to a pre-cost benefit analysis?	☐	☐	☐
f.	Is there a coherent approach to promotion?	☐	☐	☐
g.	Are attractive, effective PR materials used, and does the college have a clear visual identity?	☐	☐	☐
h.	Is the image adaptable to circumstances, and are there distinctive brand identities for niche services?	☐	☐	☐
i.	Is the best use being made of appropriate selling techniques, including direct mail, advertising and press coverage, telemarketing and presentations?	☐	☐	☐
j.	What specific action is needed to reach groups under-represented in the college and those with learning difficulties and/or disabilities?	☐	☐	☐
k.	Are senior managers involved in media relations?	☐	☐	☐
l.	Is there strong liaison with schools?	☐	☐	☐
m.	Is the college an active participant in the community?	☐	☐	☐
n.	Does the college have effective liaison with employer clients, and does it participate in TEC activities, and those of business groups, such as the chamber of commerce?	☐	☐	☐
o.	What are the levels of repeat business, and could they be improved?	☐	☐	☐

Chapter 7

Organising, Planning and Resourcing

Introduction

7.1   The organisational and administrative systems which characterise marketing in colleges vary considerably. This is not in itself a cause for concern. More important is a set of principles which need to underpin the way marketing is interpreted and implemented.

Policy Considerations

7.2   The following key issues need to be taken into consideration.

- organise the marketing function so that responsibility for student recruitment, external liaison, curriculum development, quality assurance and student services is clear, to staff and to students

- employ specialist staff with appropriate qualifications and experience, reporting to a senior college manager.

Guidance

The Marketing Function

7.3   Most colleges now have a specialist central marketing unit, although these tend to be limited in size and few employ more than five full-time staff. All have a significant involvement in the development of publicity, advertising, and in media and public relations. Thereafter the scope of the marketing function varies widely. In some cases, marketing units take the lead in market research, external liaison, pricing, service development and so on. In some cases, colleges have large central admissions units which deal with enquiries and the processing of applications, as well as publicity and PR. At all events, it is clear that there is no single organisational structure that guarantees an effective marketing approach.

7.4   Marketing manager posts in further education can be quite modestly paid, and largely preoccupied with the operational. Alternatively, a minority are members of the senior management team, take a strategic role and are paid accordingly. A number of colleges appear to organise the marketing function quite effectively, even though the word 'marketing' does not feature within the titles of any senior posts. Whatever the job title, it is important that the relevant postholders are outward-looking and show a market-led commitment to service development.

7.5   The majority of marketing staff in further education colleges tend to have been recruited from within the system and relatively few of them possess formal qualifications in marketing. There is, however, an increasing tendency to recruit marketeers from outside education. In addition, staff development and training opportunities are increasingly available for those seeking relevant professional qualifications. Annex B provides more details.

7.6   Marketing success is usually connected with the employment of marketing personnel who are chosen for their expertise in understanding customers, rather than for their specialist and technical knowledge of the service.

Job descriptions

The following is adapted from the job description for the marketing manager post in a Yorkshire and Humberside college.

Purpose

To be responsible for all marketing activities and assist in developing, monitoring and evaluating the marketing strategy.

Duties

(i)   **maintain appropriate marketing information databases**

(ii)   **develop and maintain links with industry, employers and schools**

(iii)   **establish and ensure the maintenance of a common profile for all college publicity material, and co-ordinate its production**

(iv)   **establish contact with local press, radio and national trade magazines to support internal systems of collecting and disseminating newsworthy information**

(v)   **establish a policy for college advertisements and evaluate their effectiveness**

(vi)   **arrange a programme of events and exhibitions and evaluate their effectiveness**

(vii)   **ensure that marketing expenditure is contained within the agreed marketing budget**

(viii) **actively contribute to the development of quality improvement programmes**

(ix)   **participate in appraisal programmes including the appraisal of staff as allocated to the unit**

(x)   **perform any such relevant duties that the principal may reasonably require.**

Abbreviations

ALF	average level of funding
BT	British Telecommunications Limited
CP	collaborative provision
DfEE	Department for Education and Employment
DoE	Department of the Environment
ED	enumeration district (DoE classification)
EPOC	employer perception of college
FEDA	The Further Education Development Agency
FEFC	The Further Education Funding Council
GNVQ	general national vocational qualification
LA	local authority
LEA	local education authority
LMI	labour market information
MIS	management information system
NVQ	national vocational qualification
OFSTED	The Office for Standards in Education
PR	public relations
RAT	Retention Action Team
RCU	Responsive College Unit
SME	small- to medium-sized enterprise
SPOC	student perception of college
SWOT	strengths, weaknesses, opportunities and threats
TEC	training and enterprise council
VFM	value for money

Bibliography

Audit Commission and Ofsted (1993) *Unfinished Business: Further education courses for 16–19 year olds*, London, HMSO

Donovan, K (1996) 'Student Tracking' in *Developing Further Education*, Vol. 1, No. 1, Blagdon, FEDA

Institute for Employment Studies (IES) (1997) *Identifying and Addressing Needs: A practical guide*, Coventry, FEFC

McDonald, MHB (1995) *Marketing Plans: How to prepare them, how to use them* (third edition), Oxford, Butterworth-Heinemann

NAO (1997a) *Further Education Colleges in England: Strategies to achieve and manage growth*, London, TSO

NAO (1997) *The Management of Growth in the English Further Education Sector* London, TSO

Index

Printed in the United Kingdom for The Stationery Office
J42887   C65   4/98   19585